Prepositions

Susan Iannuzzi and Peter Bushell

Longman

Picture dictionary on page 37

Parents and Teachers

Language research shows that children learn faster when they have fun. The **Longman English Playbooks** series is designed to activate children's natural curiosity and learning ability with clear, memory-fixing activities, strong, visual identification of words, scenes and actions, and an engaging, fun style. The language taught in this series has been carefully selected to match young learners' cognitive abilities and interest levels.

Longman English Playbooks are a fun and easy way for your child to start learning English together with you. This book will teach your child how to use prepositions in a sentence.

Your child will enjoy learning if you take time to show an interest in what he or she is doing. Give your child plenty of praise and encouragement. Explain any activity that your child finds difficult, and stop if he or she becomes tired or loses interest. Please check that your child understands the symbols below.

 The children trace the lines, letters or words.

 The children circle the correct words or sentences.

 The children write the words.

 The children match the words and pictures.

Trace.

in

in

on

on

under

under

above

above

Write and match.

above

above

in

under

on

2

Trace.

in front of

in front of

behind

behind

next to

next to

between

between

Write and match.

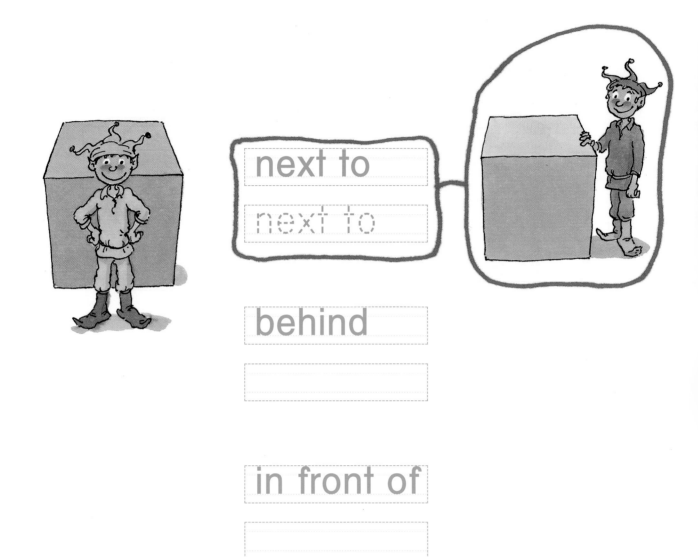

next to

next to

behind

in front of

between

Circle and write.

in

(on)

next to

`on`

under

on

above

behind

between

in

in front of

under

next to

Circle and write.

on
above
next to

in front of
between
on

above
behind
between

between
next to
above

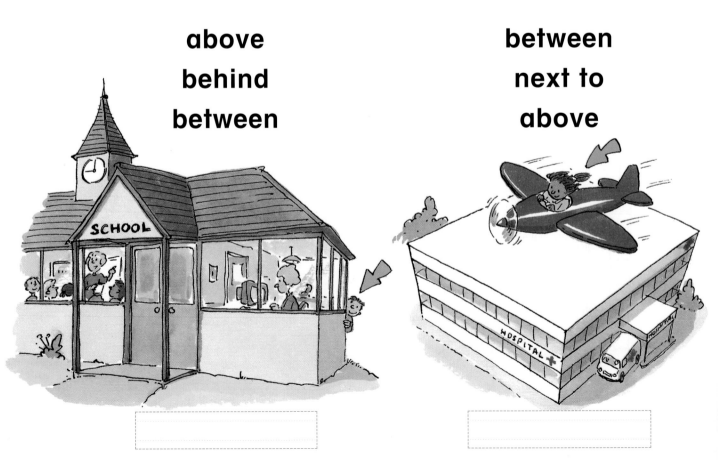

Match.

Ann   **Tom**   **Ben**   **Sue**   **Dan**

Ben

Sue

Dan

Tom

Ann

Trace.

Ann	Tom	Ben	Sue	Dan
Ann	Tom	Ben	Sue	Dan

Ann is next to Dan.

Ann is next to Dan.

Tom is behind Ben.

Tom is behind Ben.

Ben is in front of Tom.

Ben is in front of Tom.

Trace.

Sue is between Dan and Ben.

Sue is between Dan and Ben.

Ann is on Tom.

Ann is on Tom.

Tom is under Ann.

Tom is under Ann.

Sue is above Dan.

Sue is above Dan.

Ben is in the box.

Ben is in the box.

box

9

Trace and write.

school   restaurant   bridge   bank

school   restaurant   bridge   bank

school

Write and match.

Ann is in the bank.

Ann is in the bank.

Tom is on the bridge.

Tom is ____ the _____.

Dan is under the bridge.

Dan is _____ the _____.

Sue is in front of the school.

Sue is _____ of the _____.

Ben is next to the restaurant.

Ben is _____ the _____.

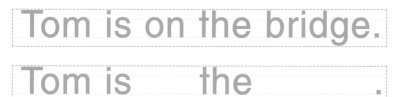

Trace and write.

| supermarket | hospital | post office |

| supermarket | hospital | post office |

hospital

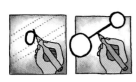 **Write and match.**

Tom is between the hospital and the supermarket.

Tom is between the hospital and the supermarket.

Ann is above the post office.

Ann is   the   .

Sue is behind the post office.

Sue is   the   .

Ben is in front of the supermarket.

Ben is   the   .

13

 **Write.**

The restaurant is in front of the _____.

Ann is _____ the supermarket.

Sue is _____ the school.

The hospital is _____ the restaurant.

The post office is _____ the supermarket and the bank.

Tom is _____ the bridge.

Dan is _____ the bridge.

The bank is _____ the post office.

Ben is _____ the school.

The supermarket is _____ the post office.

Write.

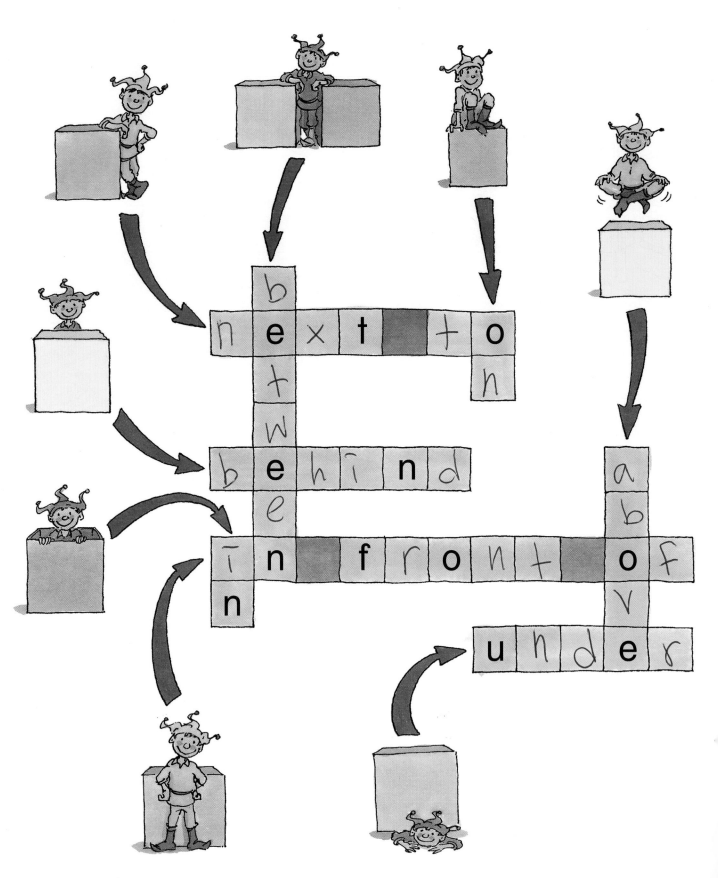

Trace.

up

up

down

down

into

into

out of

out of

17

Write and match.

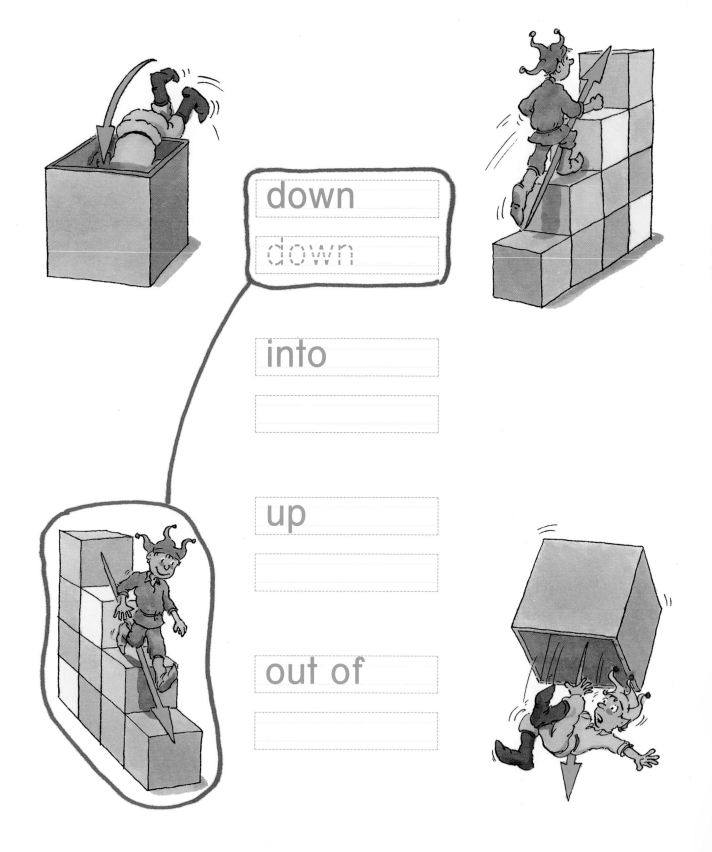

down

down

into

up

out of

18

Trace.

across

across

around

around

over

over

through

through

Write and match.

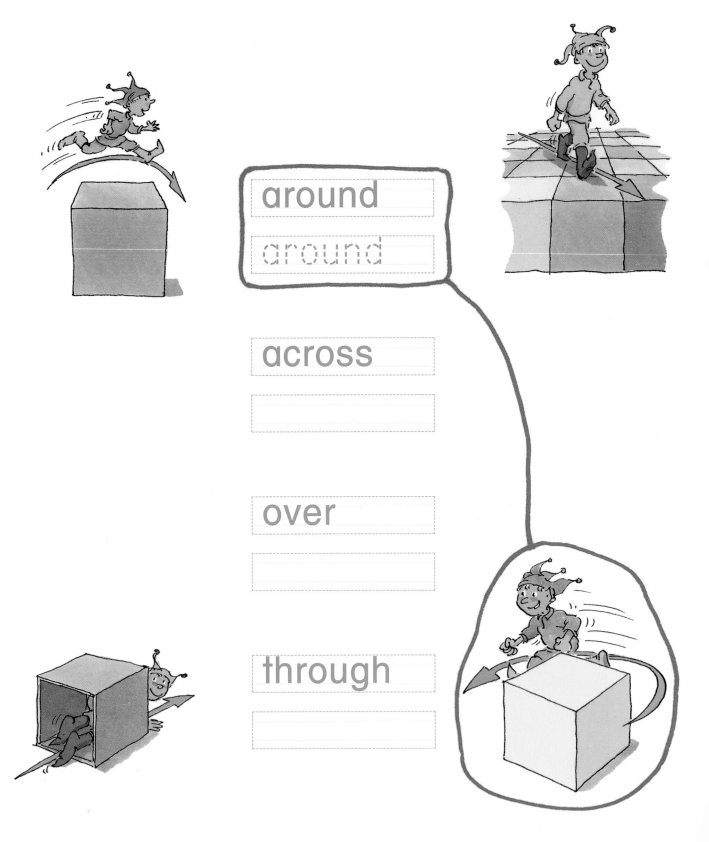

around

around

across

over

through

Circle and write.

down
up
through

around
over
through

out of
into
across

across
down
out of

Circle and write.

down
across
round

----

through
out of
into

----

through
over
down

----

out of
up
around

Write.

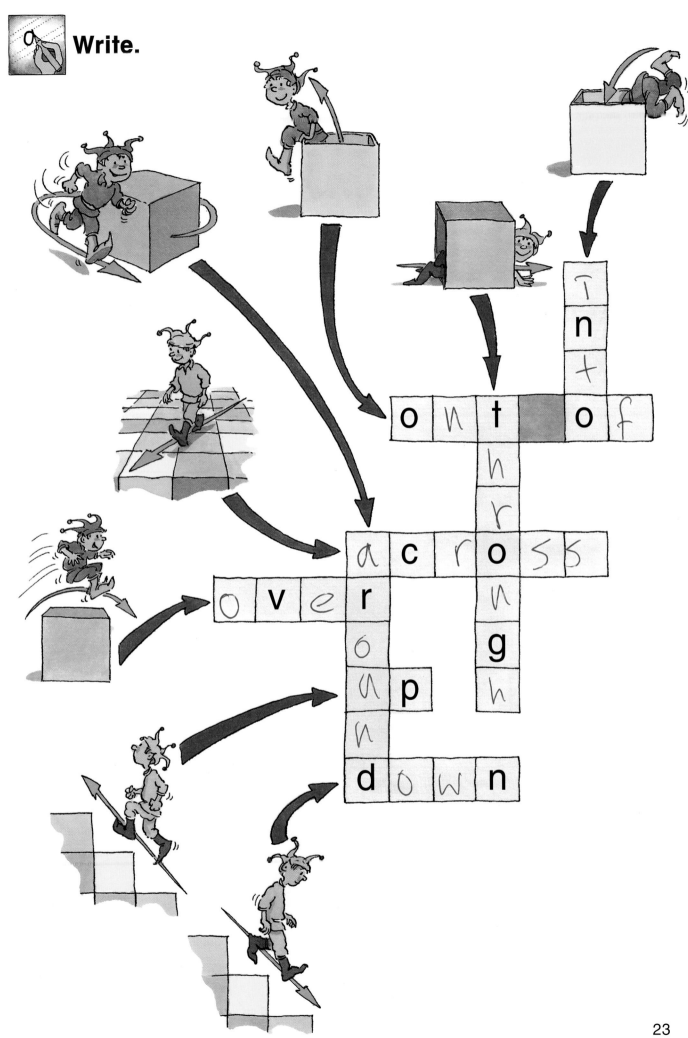

Crossword puzzle entries:
- out of
- Into
- through
- across
- over
- around
- up
- down

Trace and write.

stream   hotel   window   pool

strea   hotel   window   pool

hotel

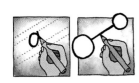 **Write and match.**

Sue is going over the stream.

Sue is going over the stream.

Tom is going out of the pool.

Tom is going _____ the _____.

Ann is going into the hotel.

Ann is going _____ the _____.

Ben is going through the window.

Ben is going _____ the _____.

Trace and write.

corner

stairs

street

corner

stairs

street

corner

26

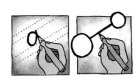 **Write and match.**

Dan is going up the stairs.

Dan is going up the stairs.

Ben is going around the corner.

Ben is going _____ the _____.

Ann is going across the street.

Ann is going _____ the _____.

Tom is going down the stairs.

Tom is going _____ the _____.

Write.

Tom is going up the stairs.

Ben is going _____ the pool.

Dan is going _____ the stream.

Ann is going _____ the corner.

Sue is going _____ the hotel.

Write.

Ann is going through the window.

Tom is going _____ the stairs.

Dan is going _____ the street.

Ben is going _____ the pool.

Sue is going _____ the hotel.

 **Trace.**

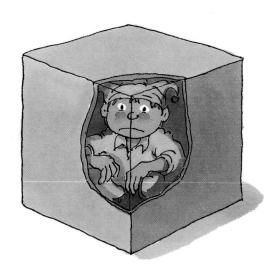

inside

inside

outside

outside

near

near

far

far

30

Write and match.

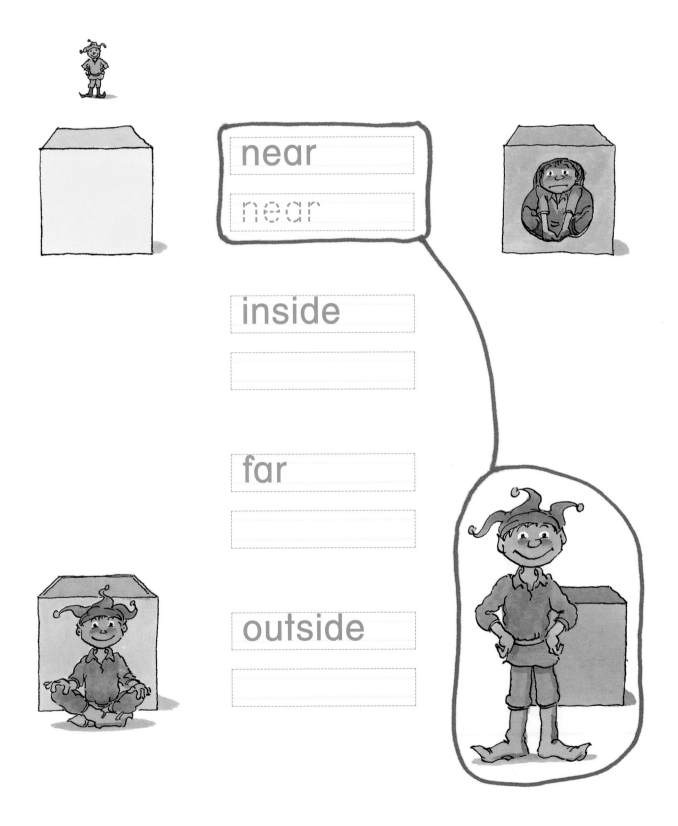

near

near

inside

far

outside

Circle and write.

far
near
inside

near
far
inside

outside
far
inside

near
inside
far

 **Write.**

Trace and write.

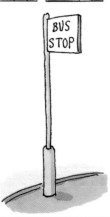

bus stop

bus stop

car

car

bus

bus

bus stop

Write and match.

Ben is inside the car.

Ben is   the   .

Tom is outside the bus.

Tom is   the   .

Sue is near the bus stop.

Sue is   the   .

Ann is far from the bus stop.

Ann is   from the   .

Ann is inside the bus.

Ben is _____ the car.

The bus stop is ___ from the school.

Tom is _____ the bus stop.

Dan is _____ the car.

Picture dictionary

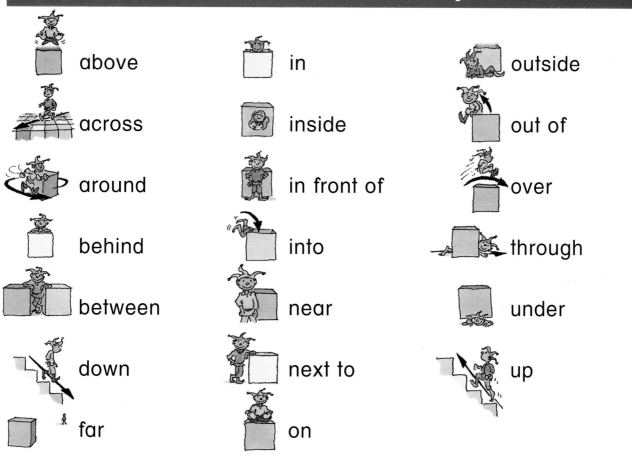

above

across

around

behind

between

down

far

in

inside

in front of

into

near

next to

on

outside

out of

over

through

under

up

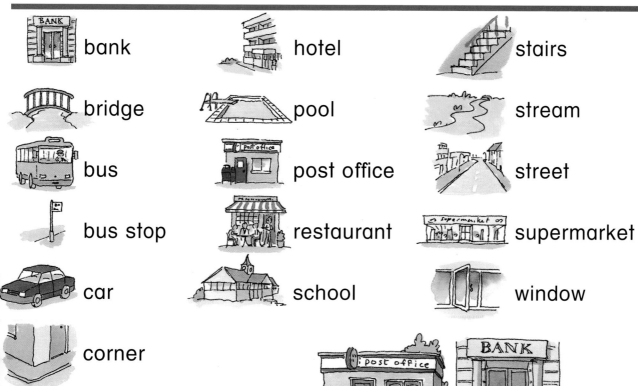

bank

bridge

bus

bus stop

car

corner

hospital

hotel

pool

post office

restaurant

school

stairs

stream

street

supermarket

window

The post office is next to the bank.

Published by
Longman Asia ELT
2/F Cornwall House
Taikoo Place
979 King's Road
Quarry Bay
Hong Kong

fax: +852 2856 9578
email: pearsonlongman@pearsoned.com.hk
www.longman.com

and Associated Companies throughout the world.

First published 1997
Reprinted by Pearson Education Asia Limited 2006

Written by Susan Iannuzzi
Illustrated by Peter Bushell

Produced by Pearson Education Asia Limited, Hong Kong
GCC/06

ISBN-13: 978-962-00-1668-4
ISBN-10: 962-00-1668-8

The
Publisher's
policy is to use
**paper manufactured
from sustainable forests**